The Eager Beaver

by Jenny Jinks

illustrated by
Giusi Capizzi

Barry lived in the forest with all the other animals. Barry always wanted the biggest and the best of everything.

He had the biggest teeth and the shiniest

coat. He lived in the biggest dam.

"But what if my dam isn't the biggest?"

said Barry. "I will build a new dam.

It will be even bigger and better."

Barry worked day and night. He cut down

lots of trees. Chop, chop, chop. He built

the dam up high.

"That is a big dam, Barry," said Bird.

"You can stop now."

But Barry was so eager he did not stop.

Barry cut down even more trees.

Chop, chop, chop.

He built the dam very wide.

"That is a very big dam, Barry," said Deer.

"You can stop now."

But Barry was so eager he still did not stop.

9

He cut, he chopped, he banged,
and he built.

"That is the biggest dam I have ever seen," said Fish. "You can stop now."

But Barry was so eager he still did not stop. He kept on building and chopping, day and night.

"Ta da!" Barry said when he had finally finished. His dam had ten storeys.

It had a games room.

It even had a swimming pool.

Nobody had a better home than he did.

Barry looked around proudly. But the forest was strangely quiet. "Where has everyone gone?" Barry said.

13

Barry went looking for his friends.

He went up and over the big hill.

Finally he found Bird.

"Why did you leave?" he asked.

"You chopped down all the trees to build your dam," said Bird. "I had no home."

"Don't be so silly," said Barry.

He didn't need Bird anyway.

Then Barry found Deer.

"Why did you leave?" he asked.

"You cut up all the bushes to build your dam," said Deer. "I had no food."

"Don't be so silly," said Barry.

He didn't need Deer anyway.

17

Then Barry found Fish.

"Why did you leave?" he asked.

"You shut off the whole river with your dam," said Fish. "There was no water left."

"Don't be so silly," said Barry.

He didn't need Fish anyway.

"They are just jealous," Barry said,

and he went home.

But he started to feel sad. He missed his friends. He had nobody to share his big dam with.

Then Barry went over the big hill and stopped.

Where was the forest?

"What have I done?" Barry said.

The forest was completely destroyed.

He had chopped it all down.

"I will put this right," he said.

And he got straight to work.

23

Barry worked day and night.

Chop, chop, chop. He didn't stop for days.

Finally Barry was finished.

He went to find Bird, Deer and Fish.

"Please come home," said Barry.

"I have something to show you."

The friends did not want to
see what crazy thing
Barry had built now.

But they went with him anyway.

Finally they made it to the top of

the big hill and stopped.

"So, what do you think?" asked Barry

nervously.

"But... your home," said Bird.

"You wanted it to be the best," said Deer.

"I already had the best," said Barry,
"the best friends."

Quiz

1. At first, what does Barry want?
a) The biggest river
b) The biggest dam
c) The biggest forest

2. What did Barry do?
a) He cut down trees
b) He found lots of sticks
c) He ate all the food

3. How many storeys did Barry's dam have?
a) Thirteen
b) Seven
c) Ten

4. Why did Barry's friends leave?
a) They didn't like the smell
b) They were jealous of Barry
c) They had no food or homes

5. What did Barry do to fix the problem?
a) He planted trees and built homes
b) He stayed inside
c) He invited his friends to dinner

Turn over for answers

Book Bands for Guided Reading

The Institute of Education book banding system is a scale of colours that reflects the various levels of reading difficulty. The bands are assigned by taking into account the content, the language style, the layout and phonics. Word, phrase and sentence level work is also taken into consideration.

Maverick Early Readers are a bright, attractive range of books covering the pink to white bands. All of these books have been book banded for guided reading to the industry standard and edited by a leading educational consultant.

To view the whole Maverick Readers scheme, visit our website at

www.maverickearlyreaders.com

Or scan the QR code above to view our scheme instantly!

Quiz Answers: 1b, 2a, 3c, 4c, 5a